The Ninetieth Day

Poems about Love, Loss, and Leftovers for Breakfast

Kristin J. Leonard

A Publication of The Poetry Box®

Editing & Book Design by Shawn Aveningo Sanders.
Cover Design by Shawn Aveningo Sanders.
Row Houses Illustration by Lucas Grey
Author Photo by Samantha Leonard

ISBN: 978-1-948461-97-9
Printed in the United States of America.
Wholesale distribution via Ingram.

Published by The Poetry Box®, December 2021
Portland, Oregon
ThePoetryBox.com

To Kelsey, Brian, Katrina,
Adrianna, Nichole, & Samantha—
Thank you for listening.

Contents

The Ninetieth Day

On the ninetieth day
the edges that held your face together
blurred. You were gone

it seemed. Then I looked to my right and saw you
in a Schultz-like gust of Pig Pen wind and dust
and squiggly lines,
        curving up and down
                and around
                        and around,
in the very place
you used to stand,
where you still stand.
Except, now—

you're devoured by deep and throaty chortles
that follow long-ago blueberry pancake mornings,
rich with the smell of bacon
spitting,
        sputtering,
                spattering,
and you poke a fork
under the pink
and flip.

You are fearless and brave and live to tell the tale
over pulp-free orange juice piled high
with ice cubes. Then you smile,
reminding me that you will live forever,
challenging the forces of the universe,

if they dare to keep us apart.
On the ninetieth day,
I was surprised to see your eyes again:

[. . .]

floating,
      Picasso-like,
           happy, I think
to be free of your face;
the fixed boundaries of edges and lines and hills and
    valleys,
the fleshy cheeks that flush orange and red and pink and
    peach
in the cool October air.

Each iris,
dark and lovely and lonely,
forms an alliance
with the side-by-side eyelashes perched above.
Thick and obedient, they blink:
once, twice, three times, then

disappear
over muted purple foothills
and the fine line that separates sunset
from 101 South. I am closer, but still ten miles away
from home.

I am in the passenger seat, I'm not sure how.
I am watching your mouth, marveling
at the words that tumble,
      fumble, and spill,
          falling forever off your tongue,
               over your lips,

evaporating into the pink pine-scented Christmas tree
that dangles from the overhead rear-view mirror,
swinging back and forth.

On the ninetieth day you rewrote the rules, no doubt—
you found a way into my early morning, *I'm-not-ready-to-
get-up-for-another-two-hours* dream.

I don't care.
I'm happy to see you;
your lips curling upwards, punctuated
by an either-side dimple standing sentry.

You whisper the punchline to a joke I never understood
the first time.
I forget how to put the parts together until eight hours pass
by and you blink at me from behind a squeezy plastic
bottle of
          Aunt Jemima maple syrup

          in the breakfast aisle at Safeway.

The Third Weekend

He was the storm that swept without warning
when we arrive late
squished elbow to elbow in the back seat
of mother's green Datsun
on the third Saturday of the month.

We wait, noses smooshed to glass
backpacks stuffed with bubble gum, pajamas
excited to see Dad's new puppy
eat chocolate ice cream
topped with sprinkles
scooped into big bowls, except
I knew he wouldn't be there
even as Mother pulls into the Albertsons parking lot
one street away from the house we used to share.

He was the breeze that settled after the rains passed
lifting a handful of leaves in an afterthought
its fury silenced. He rakes the stragglers off the driveway
while the almost-blind, no-longer-a-puppy Australian
    Shepard
            follows at his heels.

I can't wait till July he says,
remembering the three of us will visit
            for a no-longer-court-ordered vacation.

Then he sits back down at the kitchen table
and drinks another sip of decaffeinated coffee
            and talks to a parrot named Charlie.

He was the stillness in the evening air that comes before
morning,
long after the storm drifted away.

Five minutes, Dad. I'll call you right back—
And I *meant* to call him back, just as
        I meant to visit, but

He is far away, much farther than
a quick trip to Walmart
for diapers, dog food, cough syrup
and two hours later, I am unloading the groceries
when I remember
        Dad is waiting.

I tuck the baby to sleep
pour Purina in the puppy's dish
        and he picks up on the first ring.

I apologize, but he interrupts
and tells me not to worry—
he will always wait.

Words

Nestled

between breath and sound,

like old lovers and childhood,

WORDS

eventually

Die

The Precipice

I am standing at the edge
waiting for the elevator
to carry me UP
to the second floor
away from the gift shop
away from St. Joseph's emergency room
where they carried you away on a stretcher
on the Thursday I forgot my phone.

Looking
DOWN
the door to the elevator
is one inch from my toes—
one step
one nudge
one glide
one exhale, till I will be carried

UP
to the other side
to the second floor
to the precipice of life or death
to the ICU where
I will know whether you, wrapped in white
have been sentenced, not-so-suddenly
to life on the other side.

DOWN
brightens
but I still need to go UP
to where you are
to life or death or the in-between
that lies at the ICU

DOWN
the hall from the elevator
where entry is gained
by announcing my presence
my importance, and proving
I am needed
in the private room to the right
where the smell of disinfectant tingles my nose

—Patient's name?
I will waiver when they ask,
teetering too close to the edge
of knowing
of tasting
the future that might come too soon
                              if it comes
when it comes
underneath the overhead light of the ICU

UP
glows
the doors pull open
I step inside

One minute and twenty-five-seconds later
I step
OUT
onto the second floor
where the air is thin
I know I am standing
on the edge of the precipice which is
            covered with yellow speckled linoleum.

Checked "Yes"

With the strictest obedience to Truth
she filled in the details, hopeful
she found a solution to
It Was Just One Time.

After all, if she lied
—oh, how many times had she tried this before
they would find out, but
it was different this time
She had a sense that this was the opportunity
the job, or if not the job
the training
to give her the skills to do the job

Setting aside doubt
she beleaguered
down
swallowing the possibility of "No"
with the black ink pen
provided by the perfumed clerk
sitting behind the desk. Still
she believed there was a way to overcome
It Was Just One Time, so

in faith, her right hand
followed the practiced path
thoughts fixed on the possibility of 9 to 5
on a bank account balance in double digits,
her name printed on a mailbox.

She dreamed, too
of filling her grocery cart without
counting cans of green beans and cereal
of buying baby food with cash

[. . .]

when her food card expired
at the end of the month

It would take the perfect combination
—this she knew
the right day
the right time
the right place
the right opportunity, still
she focused on *maybe*

her hand racing down the page
filling in spaces
down
and down
and down
and down
until she arrived at the bottom, where

the very last box—
the one she must check "Yes"—
sent her back to

It Was Just One Time and
the one-half of a gram she
could never move beyond

Six O'clock

bright sparkles of early morning sunlight
bounce   through our open window

settling

finally,
on the pillow
                    beside me

the happy streams of polka dots bid me
good morning

then *kiss* your sleepy eyes.

On the Corner of 16th Street & Bethany Home

I w a t c h,
towering above
stucco boxes. A deep-rooted
memory *AWAKENS*; gnarled, course, ageless
when once upon a time slender blades of meadow grass
SHIVERED, back *bending* into the autumn breeze. To the
south, the long, lonely desert waits, *an ocean of sand—*
splattered with **tumbleweeds**. The wind whips north and
south and west, yet always returns here, to mountains of
grey, where green brothers once clustered, their *long limbs*
WIGGLING in the **whispering** breeze, before They arrived,
with fleshy appendages gripped to SHOUTING blades—
when *twisted* limbs of oak and fig begged,
bent, broke, cried out and Afterwards
ASSEMBLED.
b o x e s
latching
t i g h t
lacquered
doors of
s a n d ed
D O U G
LAS FIR

& P I NE

The House on Peltoma

The sky was grey on the day we arrive,
a softish grey, an almost bone colored beige
that shifts as blurbs of cottony clouds pass—
the smooth underside of a dove's wing
still pretending to be blue.
But whether blue or grey, it does not matter.
I am home. It is a holiday

on Main Street. Fresh asphalt smother
two centuries of tracks, hooves, footprints;
drapes of red, white, and blue
hang in happy folds
from storefronts, painted, polished,
ready for celebration,
holding on to the possibility that a breeze
might still remember to come.

The landlord's daughter,
almost a decade before,
invited us to take a peek at the blue room.
I hear rocking at night, she whispered
Hush. No stories—my landlord scolded

I think of home;
the smell of shortbread, Sunday roast,
planks, polished and sturdy
underneath my toes.
I never did hear ghostly rocking in the blue
room, but stayed awake many a night,
listening to

the wind push against the barn door,
a secret passageway, sealed shut,
hidden from the unfriendly eyes

of nineteenth-century visitors past
a tunnel where tired feet
caked with dried Southern mud were
always welcome, a northern respite
on the way to Canadian freedom.

On moonless evenings, I would hear
footfalls of some long-dead specter who
still had reason to avoid the front door.

I drive past Main Street,
eager to see that old house on Peltoma,
and Main Street takes no notice
of me and mine;
of dog or daughter or
the suitcase in the trunk.

The street is draped in parade best—
I look for my house:
the painted grey Victorian
that rests beside its crackly neighbors
all laced up in yellow and blue,
forever watching the passersby
who've changed only slightly
over days and decades.

I turn the corner, expecting to see
my old house on Peltoma
but there is only
a patch of dirt and gravel,
a tired fence,
a patch of green,
and a row of trees still stretching
their branches towards the sky.

I remember—
the rocking in the blue room,
the planks that bump,

I look around, at what is left:
the patch of dirt
the slant of fence
the leaves that rustle in a passing
breath of air, and I realize

I am not the only one
without a home.

Back to Bed

Standing in front of the mirror
in a patch of early morning sunlight, I realize
I've spent half my life
fussing over folds of belly fat
frustrated with dark circles that frame my eyes
bright red blemishes no cream can
conceal and

Since I'll be spending the rest of my life watching
wrinkles multiply
skin sag
feeling joints ache
lamenting, forever, the unattainable imperfection
of yesterday's Me
there's only one thing left to do: celebrate
by going back to bed.

Talking With

A gentleman traveling to Tucson told me that his sister
Talked to the dead. Between sips of Coke he confessed
She was seventy-two and chatted often with Aunt Sue who
Had been buried for decades in a cemetery

In Philadelphia. She liked to lunch
With her dead-on-arrival mother, the day she turned ten.
Of lunch last Tuesday, she confided to the gentleman
She was frustrated with her killed-in-Afghanistan brother, for

He arrived late; the waitress had already taken her order.
It began the day she woke up in the emergency room.
Under fluorescent lights, she gripped her husband's hand,
Crinkling in her blue paper gown and together

They studied the MRI image; the bulbous growth
Soon to lay claim to her blood and bones and together,
They cried and crossed off her numbered days.
Her husband mourned his soon-to-be-buried bride, but
She moved on, preferring to lunch with Mother
and gossip with Aunt Sue.

I was strapped in my seat, a captive audience,
Two thousand miles from home when
The gentleman confessed he was a bit unsettled
By his sister's conversations with the dead.

I tried to smile. I thought of you with
Your tired eyes, resting on a pillow, waiting for me.
Twelve hours passed, and I was in time to hold your hand as
Your lungs exhaled a final breath of defeat.

For you, it was past the hour of trying to hold on and
Holding it together for me. Yet no matter how I wanted,
How I watched, how I waited,
I was still sitting in the stillness
In the aftermath of you

Wondering if you, too,
Spoke to the dead as you readied yourself
To leave.

Welcome to the Catskills

They smile at me at JFK—
on a glossy brochure
on display at the information counter at
    Terminal C.

Welcome to the Catskills—
one boy, one girl, on one inner tube
their arms and legs slick with sunscreen
    pressed against one another, close enough to share

one summertime breath,
an inhale from some long, almost-forgotten breeze.
The upper edge of the brochure is curled; no doubt
hands have hovered, considering, but passed the lovers by,

selecting a glossier travel destination.
Not I. I want to sing the words aloud—
    Welcome to the Catskills

I think of taking a picture with my cell phone,
to always remember, but
        the straps on my backpack are heavy;
        the scarf on my neck, wrapped tight, to

protect me from winter on the other side of the glass.
I stand behind strangers, alone in a line that
    snakes across commercial grade carpet, zig zagging till
    it stops at
        the TSA checkpoint.

A man speaks: *It's four degrees today*—
His companion drags her suitcase,
smiles. *Still, it's almost spring*—

I think of melting snow,
of shining puddles,
dandelions, dew-dropped petals
layered in wrapped tight blossoms,
preparing to bloom without me.

I step out of line.

I need to capture the lovers
in a cell phone memory,
to set them free into cyberspace,
to defy space and time
and find their way back to you,
whispering—*Welcome to the Catskills*

Surely you will recognize them:
the boy, the girl, the innertube.
I think of this,
I reach in my pocket and touch
the American Airlines ticket wedged against
a brand-new pack of Big Red Gum.

Welcome to the Catskills

I glance at the brochure
one last time and I remember,
we already said goodbye
…to the Catskills.

Leftovers for Breakfast

She follows
with two narrow slices of green
eyes twice sliced, melting
into the backyard meadow she calls jungle.

She considers the situation
the distance
the strategy
the prize

waiting
with dilated pupils
listening for the just-right moment

to spring low
to rise forward, claws out
extending, extracting
accelerating towards her prey

Deed done
she returns to her lair,
her tail high,
holding steady

resolved
to wait in the kitchen
her contribution to breakfast
squirming in her teeth

And then the bathrobe arrives
and a cup falls, spilling
a brown liquid that splatters
across   a   patch   of   early   morning   sunshine.

T-Mobile Time

it rings four times

then silence

I speak, setting my voice free
to sail past the snow-flocked pines of Maine
the rising tide of the Mississippi
and the barren Arizona desert
that rips us apart, except
for the words, safely memorialized
in T-Mobile time

please leave me a message after the beep

When You're Going through Hell

drive fast

faster than you think is possible
in your dented Kia Rio
and don't be surprised
when the engine pushes on
without exploding ... 85, 90, 95, 100
have you forgotten?

you're in Hell, after all

nothing explodes
nothing changes

the only way to get through

is focus on the road
watch for the exit
that might exist
if it exists
at least you hope it exists
under the cloak of midnight

focus on your fingers, gripped tight to the steering wheel

focus on your destination
your direction
maintain speed, purpose, patience

fight the urge to stop

to look back
for there's nothing there, only
abyss; thick and dark and deep

swollen with shadowed memories
of brighter days

because you're in Hell, but

hold tight, for in time
you'll open your eyes to sunshine
stretching through your bedroom window
and realize the impossible,
wasn't and

you can make it through

Hell.

Acknowledgments

Many thanks to the editors of these publications for believing in and publishing these poems.

Borrowed Solace: "The Ninetieth Day"

Poets Unlimited: "Checked 'Yes'"

The Story Hall: "Words," "The House on Peltoma," "Back to Bed," and "When You're Going through Hell"

Maine's Best Emerging Poets 2019 Anthology: "The Third Weekend," "The Precipice," and "Welcome to the Catskills"

Praise for The Ninetieth Day

There is more life within these pages than many people endure in their own lifetimes. An abundance of unexpected moments is masterfully intermixed with the familiar, all of which comes from deeper than the heart, because it emanates from the vast experiences of a sagacious, ageless soul. And luckily this brilliant poet has a superb knack for verse, wordsmith ingenuity, cadence, and style. Those skills are coupled with a superior nuanced language that perfectly matches the content, topics, themes, and mood, thus delivering plenty of thrills that delight and poignant introspections that resonate.

—David E. Grubb, poet

I read poetry for its sonic appeal and impression of a story. Leonard strikes notes of Gluck, Olds, and Piercey. In most of the pieces in this collection, the woman is indeed running screaming from the burning house, but she lets you up for air with a quiet one just when you need it. I have added Leonard to my favorites.

—Shellie Leger, author of *Back Kingdom Road House*

Kristin Leonard's debut chapbook is packed with poetry that is, in turn, reflective and searching. Her unassuming, honest, heart-felt verses draw from a deep well of a full, well-lived life that keeps moving in a quest to make sense of it all. Readers come face-to-face with the tough questions, and sometimes answers, we all contemplate as Leonard navigates through the intimate maize of loves, heartaches, and losses of our

[. . .]

humanity. Like a conversation over coffee with a good friend, you'll come away from these poems with a sense that someone else understands just how you're feeling.

—Kathryn M. Balteff, MA, MFA
instructor, Southern Maine Community College

She had me at *leftovers for breakfast,* and the collection serves up tastebud surprises that will startle readers out of habitual stupors. Leonard's poem "On the Corner of 16th Street and Bethany Home" serves up begging figs that will sharpen your eyes faster than espresso, even while mesmerizing your mind with potential but uncertain meanings. In "Checked Yes," the slim remainder of *one-half of a gram* leaves your own stomach empty and lurching for fairness. The *smell of shortbread* lingers in a house since demolished, for both the living and the unrelated, long-walking dead. These poems remind us that our lives are irrevocably made possible through the ingested deaths of others, and we can think of ourselves as those leftover—serving as someone else's sustenance come the new day.

—Sid Sibo
Neltje Blanchan Memorial Writing Award Winner

Kristin's poetry is the morning sunlight you've forgotten to notice with its fun forms and wordplay sending reminders of how even the smallest things in life can breathe meaning into love, loss, and family. A wonderful little rumination on life and death and everything in between.

—Darcy Casey, author

About the Author

 Kristin J. Leonard is an adjunct college instructor that resides in Maine. She is a proud mother (of both children and chihuahuas) and looks forward to summer vacation, when she'll finally have the opportunity to dig in her garden. She holds an MFA in Creative Writing (Fiction) from University of Southern Maine, an MA in English (Literature), and a Graduate Certificate in Rhetoric, Writing, & Digital Media Studies from Northern Arizona University, where she is also completing doctoral studies in Education.

Her critical and creative work have appeared in *The Explicator*, *The Atlantic*, *Postcolonial Text*, *The Ekphrastic Review*, and more. She is the 2019 recipient of the Maine Literary Award for Drama, the 2019 recipient of Meetinghouse Theatre Lab's Maine Playwright's Award, and Lit Fest's 2019 Dramatic Writing Fellow for Emerging Writers. She is currently working on yet another revision of her first novel, an historical fiction that takes place during the housing crash of 2007. On most mornings, she can be found typing away at her kitchen table, still struggling to find the right word.

About The Poetry Box

The Poetry Box® is a boutique publishing company in Portland, Oregon, which provides a platform for both established and emerging poets to share their words with the world through beautiful printed books and chapbooks.

Feel free to visit the online bookstore (thePoetryBox.com), where you'll find more titles including:

Excoriation by Rebecca Smolen

Dear John— by Laura LeHew

World Gone Zoom by David Belmont

The Catalog of Small Contentments by Carolyn Martin

Gaslight Opera by Gary Percesepe

A Shape of Sky by Cathy Cain

What We Bring Home by Susan Coultrap-McQuin

What She Was Wearing by Shawn Aveningo-Sanders

Sylvan Grove by Barbara A. Meier

Exchanging Wisdom by Christopher & Angelo Luna

Protection by Michelle Lerner

The Fog by Mary C. Florio

Building a Woman by Deborah Meltvedt

and more . . .